To Zach: For your curiosity,
determination, and free spirit.
—DA

To Zulema, who means so much to me.
—AO

Text © 2025 by Deb Adamson
Illustrations © 2025 by Airin O'Callaghan
Cover and internal design © 2025 by Sourcebooks

Sourcebooks and the colophon are registered trademarks of Sourcebooks.

All rights reserved.

The full color was created using traditional media: watercolor, gouache, and colored pencils.

The characters and events portrayed in this book are fictitious or are used fictitiously. Any similarity to real persons, living or dead, is purely coincidental and not intended by the author.

All brand names and product names used in this book are trademarks, registered trademarks, or trade names of their respective holders. Sourcebooks is not associated with any product or vendor in this book.

Published by Sourcebooks eXplore,
an imprint of Sourcebooks Kids
P.O. Box 4410, Naperville,
Illinois 60567-4410
(630) 961-3900
sourcebookskids.com

Cataloging-in-Publication Data is on file with the Library of Congress.

Source of Production: 1010 Printing Asia Limited, Kwun Tong, Hong Kong, China
Date of Production: October 2024
Run Number: 5041065
Printed and bound in China.
OGP 10 9 8 7 6 5 4 3 2 1

A THANK YOU LETTER TO MY HOMESCHOOL

WORDS BY DEB ADAMSON

PICTURES BY AIRIN O'CALLAGHAN

I am thankful for my homeschool.
Because with homeschool, I'm free to be me!

Homeschool is not just at home or in a classroom.

It takes me on adventures—

I'm thankful for road trips.

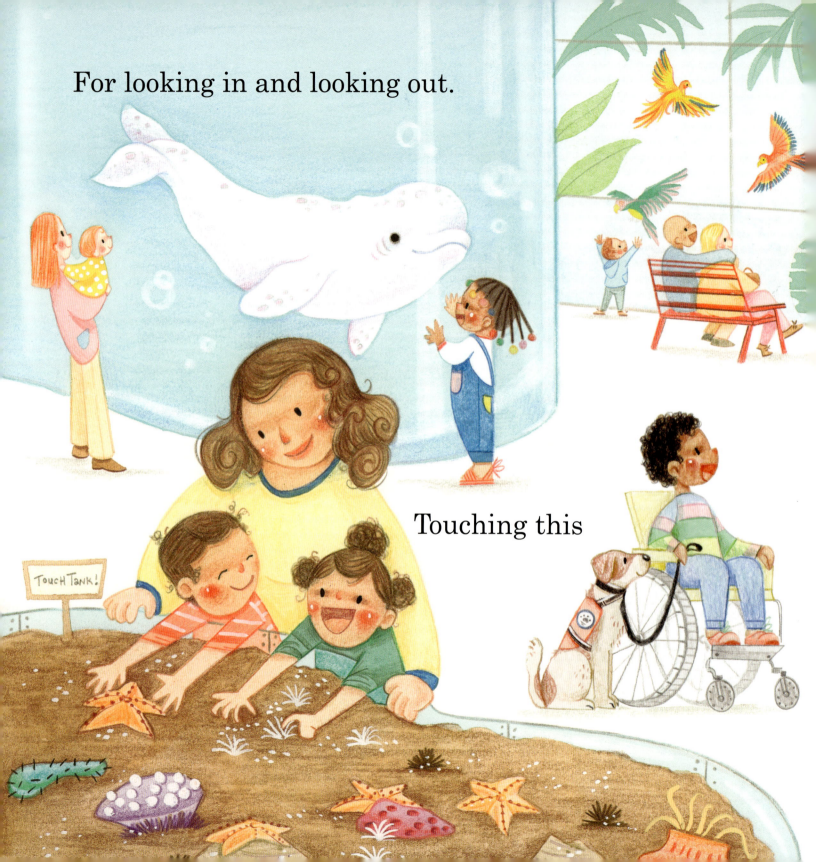

For looking in and looking out.

Touching this

and pretending to be that.

I'm thankful for days at the farm, feeding furry friends.

For gazing out from the tip-top of a lighthouse.

For standing at the feet of a giant *T. rex*.

I'm thankful for quiet days.
Cuddles on a cold afternoon,
steeped in faraway lands.

And for extra time to figure out the tough stuff.

I'm thankful for all the ways homeschool helps me grow.

Sowing,

waiting,

wondering, and watching.

Collecting and counting.

Mixing, matching, discovering.

I'm thankful for the time it gives me to invent. Building up, tearing down, and starting all over again.

Asking questions and unlocking new answers.

I'm thankful for treasured teachers

and passion projects.

For making new friends.

And sampling different tastes.

For soaring to new heights.

Splashing,

dashing,

jumping,

spinning.

I'm thankful that every homeschool day is

as different as each snowflake.

And that I am always free to be…

Me!